Words over Love

By

Jan Hamshoro

Herstellung und Verlag: BoD – Books on Demand, Norderstedt

Proofreader: Nicole Klappert

3rd Edition August 2023

ISBN: 978-3- 7543 -7786-4

**Dedicated to**:

My friend,
the one, who provided me with a pen and paper to write.

My Love,
the one and only, who inspired me with feelings to write.

"Little children, let us love, not in word or speech,
but in truth and action."

1 John 3,18

Prologue:

O my Love!

Read my words!

You might like them, you might hate them

You might enjoy them, might be disturbed by them

You might learn something, you might know them
already

You might be surprised, you might be bored

You might be all of that, yet you might be none of that

You might be me

Who am I to talk to you people about Love?

I'm simply a human

one who found the light of Love

as many of you did

one who decided to share some words of it

with all of you!

And of all these possibilities, I ask you for one

Read my words

with an open heart!

Hypocrisy

Hypocrites we are, all of us. Day and night we are and even in our Love. That is a sin and with my own sin I start, me... A human.

How come that a human can be a Hypocrite in the presence of the almighty feeling of Love? How can he be a disturbing being to the blissful pulse of life?

We are the victims of our own, with the strings of lies we draw around our lives and the lives of our closest, the lies which eventually will wrap themself around our necks and stop the air of life and love, the lies which we are spreading or not yet telling, but deep down we live by them!

And I... I'm the one who promised us a future in a small hut on a hill far away, far from the cities and people and high it should've been, next to a cliff, which would be hugging the sea and its waves.

But a Hypocrite I am, since I sold that piece of land, since I've burned all of the woods and tossed the door over the cliff and since I've stopped holding that future in my heart.

The sky is no longer blue, but full of grey. Those are clouds shaped like our pains, the heavy thunder sounding like our noisy mourning and the rain like our warm tears falling down.

Haven't you seen that storm yet? Haven't you listened to your heart? So why do we lie and say: The sky is blue! Be honest, O human, whenever you're asked!

For a long time now, my sky has been grey!

I miss the sun and the spring, I miss a clear blue day.

Shame on us! We who commit our sin with intent and keep on doing it.

Have you, human, ever heard of a strange kind of Hypocrisy? That which holds us in the nightmare of yesterday, the frightening of tomorrow and the lostness of today. That which leads us to become prisoners of Love, after we were the freest of all.

Of that Hypocrisy I tell you,

it could be the smile we face life with while having a dark hell inside our souls,

it could be the long shower we take while being drawn into the ocean of our life, it could be hearing a classical masterpiece of music but not enjoying it over the loud screams inside our heads.

Could be the new one, after our one has left, yet in life there is only the One!

Aye! We Hypocrites!

Forgiveness I seek, in the name of Love, for I have been drawn into my sins when I became what I despise, what I hate in people.

Salvation I seek!

Don't we live enough when we become what we hate in people?

Epochs of Love

In the timeline of Love, I found the Epochs and lived them and while I still breathe, I still live through the Epochs of Love. One can say Love is life... True! And just like in life, here we see the similarity of it to Love. The first Epoch of Love might start with the first eye contact or a word, a gesture or a song, it could start with a smile or a tear traveling on a pinkish cheek, it could start with a prayer or a holy glass of shared drink. Sweet is this Epoch, as a part of heaven, ran away down to our land heart, hiding in our chest and nesting in it.

Like thieves we sneak around everything in life to have more of a person. Filled with delicious fear and wanting more, with hearts sharing delightful dances and the unbreakable smile we go to sleep with every night.

The thieves of joy we are!

Like fools we talk, a pair of children in the garden of our own passion, surrounded by many young flowers we planted with our laughters, the glory wings we draw for each other lets us fly and fly with.

The fools of Love we are!

Sweet is this Epoch, yet fast it is to end.

The following Epoch of Love might start with the first face to see in the morning, being the face of Love! The first voice to touch our hearts, in the arms of adoration. Where eyes are having a long continuous uniting, a one which cannot be disturbed by the whole world.

What is my eternity?

I say, the merging of our souls, hand on hand and eyes on eyes, chest to chest and lips hugging from time to another. A song about the hair of my love and how it could be the forest I wish to be lost in.

With poems saturated with our love, we keep seeking languages to translate what we carry within our hearts, spending the whole night and wanting more.

Aye! That is my eternity and the most precious of this Epoch. It is the golden age of our Love story.

The seeker of this eternity I shall always be.

Heartwarming is this Epoch, yet fast it is to end.

Lucky are very few, those who live not the next Epoch,

The post-Love Epoch:

This is an end before being a start, the end of joy, the end of a future. Flowers will grow in that garden no more, autumn will tear down every leaf of our beloved tree.

Yet wait for the spring, but it might be very late.

The post-Love Epoch really starts with the last goodbye. Your eyes will be generous with the tears, the heart will plunge into the spiral of pain, no peace for the chest. The mind with the heavy storm of thoughts will become a lost kid, nowhere to be found.

Suddenly the world is your pain, the roads you shared, the songs you heard, the cities you traveled to, the words you said and heard, the air you shared and the dreams you had! How could dreams hurt us?

Aye they do...

Painful is this Epoch and it lasts!

Historic monuments of Love

And the history of Love, just like the history of Humans. Full of ups and downs, golden and dark ages, with crying and laughing, rich with memories of all kinds. And through the Love we build our monuments, those we have and those we live, statues of memories to tell us a story of a pleasant yesterday. To have a nice thing through the hardness of a random day.

It could be a gift, an old book telling a story about an old couple and their farm with the barn, in the middle of nowhere, with a special kiss print on the first page.

It could be a message, written in a moment of godly Love, with massive waves of a strange feeling, with a shaking hand and with tears of joy or with shy smiles.

It could be a ticket of the last subway ride you shared before you say: Goodbye!

It could be a picture which was stolen from a random moment of time on one of your spring trips.

It could be a perfume that makes you close your eyes and smile, reminding you of a warm hug, a home.

And it could be everything in Life, every road you

shared, every song you danced to, every book you discussed, every movie you watched, every city you visited or thought of visiting, every river you crossed, every tree you hugged, every star you named, every night, every day, every word of every language you spoke to each other.

Aye! With everything in life I bind our souls!

These and many others are the stones of the temple of your Love, hold tight to them and take care of them in the name of your heart, these are the bridges to the beautiful past and the ring you shall never take off.

The presence of them creates no true pain, but rather the sweet nostalgia and nostalgia we shall have. It is the delicious drink of what was once called: Us.

The Monuments are a sandcastle we build on the shore of our lives and the anger of separation is just a wave. Let not a wave bring down a beauty you build in the time of your Love, there the wave will soon be put to rest.

Have you seen a human sabotaging their own history?

Be not the savages, those who ruin their own history, their own being in their life! Don't commit a blasphemy to your Monuments and tear down the temple.

We are what we live and once lived, what we have and once had, therefore make your peace with yourself, with the history and Love it all.

Beauty

Mortal is the Beauty which we see with our eyes and immortal is the Beauty that we have in our souls. And our Beauty of the soul we should bind.

Search not for it! Beauty could be found anywhere at any time. A colourful flower growing on a dead land, a land which suffered a war no one knows when it did start, a land which knew nothing but the ashes, blood and screaming, a land of nothing and a land where no names are remembered. Despite all that madness, you will see that pretty plant blooming.

To see that flower through all that darkness, to see the Beauty, we have to look closely, because the Beauty starts within our eyes. No Beauty would be seen with eyes not shouting of Beauty. We all have such eyes, we are all born with them, yet sometimes we catch a thin layer of mist between them and life.

Lucky are the eyes that saw the mortal Beauty and then became a key to the heavenly door of immortal Beauty of the soul. There the eye belongs to our souls, willing to give and please.

Lucky are the eyes that saw her hair floating on the sound of the flirtatious words of spring breezes.

That saw her smile, a star like no other, a great warm light of which we hear only in legendary myths.

That saw her cheeks and neck, the beautiful land where I plant my stories and those maps where I left my trace on.

That saw her eyes and got lost in them until they led the way for our souls to bind in a dance of eternity!

The beauty that we bind our souls with, we call: Adoring!

And adore I did!

Your soul and its Beauty being the sun of my days and the moon of my nights, being the serenity with which I overcome my daily madness, being the light which leads my ship away from the storm in the middle of the ocean, being the joy and bringing the happiness to my life, being the peace for the disturbing and tragic history of mine, being the gorgeous rhythm I need in my chest to live.

O human! How come you hide the joy when you have it and not share it with a world that needs it. Why do you hold it away from a world out of joy? Isn't it a nice day, the one with a smile of happiness given by you? Fear none and call your happiness, call the beauty as a prayer to those who will enjoy your words and smile.

Misery upon us! We who have hidden their happiness out of fear!

O human! How come you put an end to what could have been, an era of an eternity of Beauty. Where the Beauty might have been the first being to see in the day and the last in the night. What is more beautiful than to sleep and wake up next to the Beauty of your life? An end to that Beauty? How could you commit that sin with your own hands?

Shame on us! We who have ruined the Beauty in our own life.

Dream

Illusion of our wishes and desires, a space of our own, yet we have no control over it, but we should not be in control. A reason why the Dreams are a nice place to be. A human might say: "Dreams have no meaning" and I say: "Sightless is such a human".

In Dreams we are like children choiceless not knowing how to lie, a space of honesty with all of our thoughts, memories and visions.

And like children we can have our own mysterious world in there, with a door made of rainbow, trees out of sweet candies and rivers out of our favourite drink.

It might be a bright place where we live our ambitions as they are, ignoring the barriers of reality and humans, away from the wonder and the confusion of "What if?!". High is our sky and untouchable, unless we desire to, in the space of freedom.

Yet it also might be a dark one, with some suffering and maybe pain, fear and anxiety, it might be even harder than the ugliness of reality that we try to escape from. And that we call: a Nightmare.

O land of Dreams! You who welcome all visitors, no matter where they stand in our life and present. Kind you are to have them, those guests, who might also have left us, to give a shelter for the night. And regardless of what they offer us, pleasure or pain, you host them anyway and bring them into your play.

O land of Dreams! Tell us how we could tell apart a Dream from a nightmare, where our beloved one is playing. Is it a Dream when we enjoy it? And if so, isn't it a nightmare then that we wake up?

We always wonder what a Dream could mean, but that's not the question, we should rather wonder why we dreamed that? Why is the mind pulling this vision for us to witness, could it be a message to prepare us for the future or is it because of the nostalgia stuck in our chest? Tell us, O land of Dreams! Tell us why.

Weird are the Dreams and annoying they can also be, as if they show you what you miss in your days willingly and letting you feel helpless, as if they want you to be ashamed of the courage you are missing to make them a truth, yet maybe they are motivating you to do so.

As if they could say: O human! Be brave and fulfil us!

O holy tree! On your trunk was our assembly on a summer's day with the warm whistles of the wind tickling our cheeks, on the edge of a calm lake. A moment to last as long as life in heaven.

O tree! Holy you got to be, with our shared Love which you witnessed. So was it a Dream?

Aye, a Dream we both had, a Dream together we fulfilled.

Jealousy

Ugly and lonely monster! Living in a cave of our being and sometimes leaving his dark hole to lead a rumble when he wakes up.

With a defaced figure and grumpy face, sharp eyes empty of everything but not the fury, a great fire you carry with a deformed hand and a long chain of thorns in the other. Through the rage you are willing to find a rest, yet causing the pain is your only fate.

Like a little child he would build a huge conflict for the sake of attention and not only that he seeks. A foolish child with ignorance of the consequences of his actions in a moment of rage, that child in us leaves after the break we take of the mess he created, goes back to sleep dreaming of the next revolution and like that we are left to heal the wounds he left with his claws of anger. The faster we heal those wounds, the less we suffer, the more we are pleased!

Why are we spending a long time fighting you where we actually should just hug you? From us and for us you are, O cranky monster, born within our lives, a feeling like all other feelings.

You are ugly, but who is not, when moved by anger!

O human! Who among us is not? And lie not to me, neither to yourself. Jealous I am, was and will be!

Lucky are those who accept it as all other feelings, to take that monster and treat him like the kid he is, to calm him with the bond of trust we gain in life, to teach him about the Love and help him see more, to smile at him while he sleeps instead of having to deal with a chaos left behind.

O Jealousy!

A blessing we named you when you helped and brought

us together

A curse we named you when you helped and

tore us apart

Hope

The candle we hold in our hearts, with its flame we can see and even find comfort. A candle to light up high and that sometimes fades and gets smaller and maybe sometimes it will disappear. Have you ever seen such darkness? In which we feel nothing, care for nothing, not willing to see if there will be a sunrise tomorrow, not willing to see if there will be peace upon us, what peace and the war already destroyed everything inside of us?

Aye! We might lose that torch, the one we call Hope, yet it comes back, O human, that is in our being, so breathe life more!

The eyes of a child, riding his bike with a friend back home after a long day in the village where he spent hours playing and jumping around! The eyes with which he knows that back home, the meal is waiting for him as is his mother's hug! Pretty are his eyes and full of Hope!

Hope is not a lonely traveler, if you see it then look at its shadow and you shall see the shy companion, the one which will not leave his side. Patience is he called and separated from one another they cannot be. And patience is no easy path, neither is it a sweet one. Yet a path we must take, in order for the Hope to be. No Hope is there for us without having patience!

Careful, O human, of a Hope which after a lifetime of patience comes to reveal itself as a mirage in the desert, as if it was never there. See with your heart and mind if Hope is deceiving you and if so, overcome it even if it's a Hope.

Yet can we put this Hope to rest with a bullet of mercy? Mercy to our hopeless lives!

Go to the woods, to the mountains, to the fields, go to a blue lake or to the sea and enjoy the silence of the universe around you in the arms of nature, give yourself a moment of peace where you hear no one and see no beings, maybe the wind will whisper something into your heart, so wait there, wait for the Hope, for that it will come and complete your sentence when you say, I am alive!

Let him live within our heart, the Hope which draws us the tomorrow we are not stopping to dream of, let him grow and prosper and build his gardens, let him free. The Hope of Love!

We sleep at nights, thanks to Hope, we get to see beauty in our days, we get to dream and to wake up to a whole new day! We get to laugh, to sing and to have the pulse, we expect the sun over the grey, thanks to Hope.

O human! Hope and hope. Hope for the spring, for the sun, for a full moon, hope for a dance, for a coffee, for a play, for a song and for freedom. Hope to get lost in the arms of Love.

I believe in Hope, I live with it, write my words with it!

Regret

"Do you remember?!" A Regreter shouted, "Do you remember, O my Love, the happy city we once visited? I went back there last summer and I met Regret! The streets, those which we have not visited yet, were filled with it. A Regret of not being visited by us together. Even the streets which we walked through, holding hands, faced me with Regret, a Regret to have just me this time. What should I have told them or told the sad city? I as well... I regret that too!" I heard him say and felt his regrets.

Brave is the human who decides to face his regrets with an open heart, not letting a space for some pride to stand between his thoughts, letting the truth flow through his heart.

Let not pride deface the truth in your heart, the truth that we are creatures who regret. We humans are no greater than having our Regrets, so what for the false pride?

Life will give you, while it holds your hand through the journey, Regrets, gifts which you must take. Yet you decide what to regret when you get to make a decision, what to do and how to go, to leave the Regret of it behind.

And if you regret and you will, like me or the Regreter, then look up to the peace you shall seek to make with that Regret, there it will be for long, a play with time.

And of Regret, I tell you: Regret is every night you have spent together but did not dance through it. It is when you did not give the heavens a play to watch or the stars a joy of your Love.

And of no Regret, I also tell you: Unique is our Love, the one we are fully loyal to, even if it got to the post-Love Epoch, the cell of loneliness we chose willingly and not feeling any regrets, the small chamber surrounded by our own warm feelings, keeping us from heading towards the cold of treason. Commit no treason, O human, to your own heart, and the Love it is holding.

A cell, aye! Yet a place of freedom, beautiful and comfortable, and loyalty is what makes us the nobles and saints we should be, when we Love!

How is it possible to replace the sun with a random light? Neither warmth to be felt nor delightful to brighten our days.

You might, O human, follow a random star, far it might be or close to you, through your galaxy of life, yet you will come back with your flags down, every battle lost.

And the loyalty to your heart you shall not Regret, O human, but rather be proud of!

Blessing

A human who hides in the shadows and closes his eyes to claim there is no sunlight, who eats voraciously the fruits of a generous, wealthy and giving tree and then chops it off after filling his stomach, who yells I am and ignores the Us! Who acts ungrateful when it comes to the many Blessings of Love, he is a fool!

O human, why aren't you fighting your ego? The ego which holds you from bringing the Blessings to the light and singing them to your soul and heart. The Blessings are yours, to raise you to be higher in your life rather than staying in the place you are now. Embrace the truth and hug it. The Blessings are a part of us and of them we should be proud.

The Blessings are the poetry, the words of a legend, which hold us a tomorrow as a human with a new virtue. We, the pupils of life, gain more of ourselves.

The Blessings are the mosaic that could describe us, the humans we become after a lifetime of Love, to help us gain the missing pieces of ourselves. To be the better of I was, to become the I am.

The Blessings are uncountable and we could be surrounded by them without seeing them.

Few I shall mention and these I took with me in my small notebook of life through my beautiful journey:

Blessed I am with your being, O my Love, to hold on to my dreams and embrace my wings to fly and maybe I will touch the sky. I pity those who found no believer in their life.

Blessed I am with your being, O my Love, on the same ground as I am, where only the seas and the oceans are separating us even more. I pity those who cannot see that.

Blessed I am with your being, O my Love, to achieve the peace I dreamed of between me and my own body. I pity those who spend their life and reach nothing.

Blessed I am with your being, O my Love, to unbosom the goodness in my life, to gain the light to see the road I am on. I pity those who are burying it in their life.

Blessed I am with your being, O my Love, to be wiser than the child I used to be, like a man who left the People and went to the mountains. I pity those who are sticking to their father's thoughts.

Blessed I am with your being, O my Love, to realise the monster in me, the beast of anger who hit with a sword of scream, I pity me until I bring him to a rest and those who fight him in themselves.

Blessed I am with your being, O my Love, to love, respect and appreciate, more and more, the heavenly Eva in our lives. I despise those who are not.

Blessed I am with your being, O my Love, to have memories we made, the cosy space I have and visit to watch us in ecstasy. I pity those who are ashamed of theirs.

Blessed I am with your being, O my Love, to write words in your name, the vocabulary I'm inspired with, by the beauty of your revelation. I pity those who are lost without it.

Blessed I am with your being, O my Love! Yet cursed I am, with your absence!

Death

O human! Are you alive? Why do you think that you are alive? Our parents will not teach us a lot of things, but our great mother, which we all humans share, the one we call life, does. And if only we could understand life, then you would get to know Death more!

Death is an old friend of us humans, we have shared health and sickness, laughter and tears, wars and peace. He has been around since the beginning. A mysterious friend full of surprises, a puzzle that takes a lifetime to be solved and one day we will celebrate the last moments of life with him.

There will come a day when we get to know him better and have him in our lives and yet keep breathing life, there Death could come with many different faces, in such a day he will disguise.

One particularly hideous face, I shall share its horror with you. A face that haunts me even in my most peaceful days, a face which steals my dreams away and throws me into the long nights, a face which is having me hanging between the sky and the land of nowhere, not knowing if I am alive or gone.

Death, where your heart gives up beating, is something we might say lies not in our hands, something you can't change. But a Death wearing the mask of separation is one, just like sins, made by us. One we can undo, yet we are not changing it.

Separation is hard and full of misery, not having the joy we once had, it makes us strangers to our own selves, it makes us incomplete in a way and not like the humans we were.

Do you call it a life after the loss of the great bridge two lovers once had between them? And what kind or quality of such a life can we see through it?

Tell me what do we call this life if it's our bridge that collapsed, if it was our beautiful garden that was conquested, if it's our entangled hands that went departed.

Like two leaves struggling with autumn on one bough, promising each other that together they shall stay, high and where they belong, together. But autumn will have his victory and they will fall and let the wind draw them along an unexpected path. Tell me, what do you call this kind of life?

Life is no more without your smile in the morning and the whispers of your voice, without the fingers going lost in your hair, without an evening of your lovely presence with our favourite music keeping the stars from falling asleep, without holding your hand and watching the sunrise on this land.

Shame on us! We who see that Death, but not fighting it and just mourn our life.

Where did my Love go?

Far away from the place where I came to this life, not knowing yet where I would say my goodbye to it. Just a stranger in a strange world.

We have two homelands to which we belong, as long as we breathe: in one we are born and in the arms of the other we die.

Yet how come I have lost both of my homelands?